TOTAL FOOTBALL

TOTAL FOOTBALL

Jon Haynes and David Woods
(Ridiculusmus)

OBERON BOOKS
LONDON

WWW.OBERONBOOKS.COM

First published in 2011 by Oberon Books Ltd
521 Caledonian Road, London N7 9RH
Tel: +44 (0) 20 7607 3637 / Fax: +44 (0) 20 7607 3629
e-mail: info@oberonbooks.com
www.oberonbooks.com

A catalogue record for this book is available from the British
Library.

ISBN: 978-1-84943-015-9

Cover images by Vivian Cooper Smith.

THE CHARACTERS ARE PLAYED BY
TWO ACTORS AS FOLLOWS:

Actor 1
NIGEL BURTON
SIR ROGER JEFFREYS
MIGGY

Actor 2
PAKISTANI MAN
BRIAN MESSENGER
SIR ALEX FERGUSSON

Total Football was first presented by Ridiculusmus at the Pit Theatre in the Barbican Centre, London on 19 May 2011, performed by David Woods and Jon Haynes.

Created by Jon Haynes & David Woods
Design by George Tomlinson
Lighting by Mischa Twitchin
Sound by Russell Goldsmith
Choreography by Luke George

Production Manager, Andrea Salazar

Technical Stage Managers, Lee Jones & Helen Mugridge

Producer, Joanna Crowley

Assistant Producers, Katy de Main & Becki Haines

Press Associate, Elin Morgan, for Prospero

Two men wearing light grey suits. One of them (Actor 2) holding a white A4 ring binder.

SFX: Stadium.

1. THE CULT OF THE FOOTBALL MESSIAH 1

DUET: Rooney Rooney Rooney hurr Rooney hurr
Rooney hurr Rooney hurr Wayne Rooney hurr
Wayne Rooney hurr Wayne Rooney hurr Wayne
Rooney hurr Wayne Rooney hurr Wayne Rooney hurr
WayneRooneyWayneRooneyWayneRooneyWayne
RooneyWayneRooneyWayneRooneyWayneRooney.

A foootball dance routine.

The dance finishes. Actor 2 puts a ring binder in the back of a chair and moves to behind a screen which Actor 1 has set up in the black.

2. A CELEBRATION OF BRITAIN TODAY

NIGEL: An almond croissant washed down with a cappuccino made from Morroccan beans by a Canadian coffee chain… a Chinese take away sitting on Swedish furniture as you watch an American cop drama. This is what it means to be British today *(This reminds him to ring his wife.)* – Answer phone. Hi babe, it's me – just wanted to say don't tape over the hard drive – I got last night's **'Wire'** on it and didn't do the save function yet. Hey and I dunno about the coffee machine but I've been going to the toilet all morning – either that or the milk is off. Maybe chuck it and I'll get another at 7 11 on the way home – **Love ya.**

He flips down the screen (with A Celebration of Britain Today written on it) and reveals the Pakistani man, who has wandered behind the flip-up screen and remains hidden until this moment.

NIGEL: Oh sorry didn't see you there. You've come for the conference?

MAN: Yeah, yeah.

NIGEL: I'm was just going over my spiel

MAN: So is it a talk or do the audience…?

NIGEL: Well I've got a talk prepared and yeah there's time allotted for –

MAN: Discussion?

NIGEL: Yeah, for discussion at the end

MAN: Are you Nigel Burton?

NIGEL: Yeah – I'm with the DCMS – I suppose you saw that on the leaflet, did you?

MAN: *(Moving downstage to get a better view of the display banner.)* Right, you're leading the thing about celebrating Britain?

NIGEL: Yeah yeah yeah I am yeah… well it's a Celebration of Britain .. today

He has put the banner back up again.

MAN: Yes

NIGEL: it was actually originally a 'celebration of Britain' and I ermm … there was a mistake at the printers – cos I said 'today at 8pm' but they missed out the ….. – I mean that's okay but its more than just contemporary or contemporary-ist – you know it's more than that it's history it's historirical … So did you want to talk about?

NIGEL has sat in the only chair on stage. The MAN looks around for a chair and then squats.

MAN: About the topic? Yeah, I suppose what I'm interested in being a Pakistani man –

NIGEL: Fair enough.. so you were born in Pakistan but have come to live in England?

MAN: No I live in Pakistan

NIGEL: So you're just visiting? You're not here as a citizen?

MAN: I have family here

NIGEL: Yeah

MAN: But maybe I come to live here.

NIGEL: Yes

MAN: Depending on if I like what I see.

NIGEL: Well I can say as a black British man

MAN: Excuse me?

NIGEL: Coming from a family of African descendants, being black British

MAN: You're not very black

NIGEL: Well, …

MAN: I'm blacker than you

NIGEL: But you're brown aren't you?

MAN: I'm black

NIGEL: You're obviously in the sun a lot and what with the weather and everything we do tend to fade a bit. But let's not get into an I'm blacker than you – I've got more black friends than you argument – but yeah yeah descending … basically my parents emigrated to England from the Caribbean

MAN: West Indian?

NIGEL: Yes

MAN: Not African?

NIGEL: Yeah originally from Africa, like my forefathers went over to work on the sugar plantations – I say work but not in the sense of getting paid – and kind of took advantage of when the empire said you know come back to its subjects – we're running out of people, expecting the whites to come back and then got, you know…quite an handful and consequently I was born here. So my identity is mixed up with immigration and intertwined with a different story so I take your point

MAN: What?

NIGEL: That you were thinking about moving here

MAN: Yes I suppose that's why I came to this talk

NIGEL: Right.

MAN: Interested to see what this Britishness identity is about

NIGEL: Well I think its …

He stands up and moves away to ruminate.

MAN: So if I come here do I become British?

MAN moves towards the empty chair.

NIGEL: Well eventually if you chose to live here you would become British – it's your choice if you want to apply for immigration

MAN: Pass a test?

NIGEL: There is a test, you get a big book with all things like the flag, the anthem, all about the political set up – what … what's the constitution of the UK

MAN: What is the constitution of the UK?

NIGEL: Well it's sort of you know it's kind of like err. You know ….. well you know we don't have a bill of rights as such. You know we don't have a kind of document that says 'we the people'.. it's sort of the obiter dicta of the, you know, the parliamentary democratic monarchy patriarchal patriarchical .. monarchy system where the queen is basically calling up the government where the government has been formed err from the popular vote and then the government, the queen forms the government like in the movie and err.. you know but you'll learn all about that in your test you know .. I'll just go and see if anyone else is coming because we want to fill the hall and nice as it is to talk to you I want to be sure we get the numbers

MAN: Well I can't wait forever

NIGEL: Yeah I thought I might wait til twenty past

MAN: Pushing it a bit

NIGEL: I think twenty minutes would be a reasonable …

MAN: Pity if no-one else turns up

NIGEL: To be honest I don't think we'll do it if no-one else comes

MAN: Just me?

NIGEL: Yeah

MAN: Am I not good enough?

NIGEL: No you're fine… it's just not the numbers we were

MAN: You say you won't do it just for me?

NIGEL: Obviously there are overheads. Well I could do it for you, but I could just give you an information pack

MAN: Maybe I can't read it. I made a lot of effort to come here tonight

NIGEL: What's your native language? Of your country? Where you come from?

MAN: Urdu

NIGEL: I have an information Urdu pack I can give to you to take away. Indian take away

MAN: I'd rather get it first hand

NIGEL: Well I can give you an information pack

MAN: It's not the same

NIGEL: No I understand. But the event's not the same

MAN: I came for a discussion

NIGEL: Yeah we can't really have a discussion, you and I

MAN: Two people's enough

NIGEL: We can talk yeah but..

MAN: Where are you going?

NIGEL: I just thought I'd see if there are any more people coming for the discussion. *(He goes off and mutters – fucking hell – shit – fucks sake etc.)* – No one's out there yeah – essentially we're a nation of whingeing stuck up apathetic shits and this ain't gonna happen. I'll get you that pack… apathetic shits – *(He packs up the display banner and now wants the chair that the man is still sitting on.)* though we did invent the telephone

MAN: He was Scottish

NIGEL: Yeah well believe it or not that's part of Great Britain too. Innit?

He nudges the man out of the chair.

BLACKOUT.

3. LONDON WINS

SFX: Long version of Jacques Rogge announcing 'and the winner is (they look up): London' cheers.

The two leap around ecstatically but don't hug, they don't know how to – so a bit of back patting goes on but mostly its pushing away which merges into the hung heads of –

4. THE POST MORTEM INQUIRY IS LAUNCHED

BRIAN: In the aftermath of every great British sporting disaster there is inevitably a need for understanding of what went wrong, how it went wrong and why and the London 2012 soccer tournament has been no different. This morning's early day motion from the member for Southend West, and I quote, 'That this House expresses its great concern at the events of the Olympic soccer competition and calls for an urgent enquiry into the state of the national game' end quote – has tasked us at the DCMS with the challenge of supplying some answers and answers are also actually what I am desperately in need of in my private life, the clinicians having so far been unable to explain the reason for my infertility. I would like to respond at the launch of this enquiry with the words of Elizabeth Kubler Ross who described the grieving process as having five or is it seven stages which I think might be of use to us in this instance – One: Denial – we're going to win –Two: Anger – they cheated. Three: depression –. We're shit. And it's raining. Four: Acceptance – that's ok, Five: denial again – we'll win it next time, and I didn't really want to go into this again but my wife's fallopian tubes, although blocked, we were told, could be unblocked, and were finally unblocked on the same afternoon that Argentina played Britain 5 – 1 in the second week of the tournament and therefore she is now able to conceive, but most probably only with the assistance of a fertile man, in other words not me.

5 BACKWARDS IN TIME

ROGER: Regnessem nairb, Regnessem nairb, esealp eciffo ym ot ecom ouy nac. Regnessem nairb, Regnessem nairb, Brian Messenger. Brian Messenger can you come to my office please Brian Messenger?

BRIAN walks backwards to upstage right position, narrowly missing ROGER who also goes backwards pulling the middle ranking chair to stage right then arcing backwards to a football upstage centre and putting his foot on it.

6A. THE TASK

BRIAN does a circuitous route round the imagined floor of the building, ending upstage right again but with footsteps carrying on even when he has come to a standstill.

ROGER: Hi.

BRIAN: Hello.

ROGER: I'm Roger Jeffries …

BRIAN: Yes.

ROGER: I'm the Under Secretary of State for sport and the arts and culture in England. Um, I've been advised by the

Minister for Sports, the arts and culture in England, um, of a particularly sensitive confidential matter and I'm looking for a bright young enthusiastic bureaucrat to help me. *(He does a 360 to centre stage with the ball.)* I've picked you. Now this isn't an idea that the Minister's come up with, this is coming straight from the PM. We, well we think that the, the Britishness issue can be addressed by winning a gold medal in the, in the London Olympics football category by entering a UK super team – and I say this to you in confidence, well firstly, *(He dribbles backwards to initial position.)* are you, I should have said before, are you happy to sign up to this, are you happy to be the person that does this work?

BRIAN: Sorry, what work do you want me to do?

ROGER: You will be the coordinating officer on this project.

BRIAN: Coordinator of the British team?

ROGER: Yes, the Chef de Mission – *(Dribbling forwards slowly.)* Now what do you know about, what do you know about … *(Dribbles back.)* Are you happy to do it? That's the first …

BRIAN: It sounds exciting.

ROGER: Okay so if that's a yes.

BRIAN: Yes, yes.

ROGER: *(Moving downstage with football.)* Mm. Now we've chosen you because you're bright, you're young, the sort of person we want to move up in the department – and I thought, I … imagine you're interested in sport. I don't expect that to be the case, um, in a way if you're not knowledgeable about sport it might actually be of benefit so that there's no …

BRIAN: Well no, I'm not that interested in sport actually, apart from tennis and um …

ROGER: What do you know about firstly the Olympics and secondly the sport of football?

BRIAN: Well um, I know the basics about the Olympics, but I'm not a football fan, I should tell you that.

ROGER: And what do you know, what's your idea of, or knowledge of football in the Olympics?

BRIAN: Well very little really. Does it usually happen?

ROGER: Okay, so …

BRIAN: *(Moving towards ROGER and the ball.)* Is there, has there been football in the Olympics before? Before now?

ROGER: Yes there has and I think what we'll do is, *(Tackling the football away from him flicking it up and catching it.)* I'll get you to go and do some preliminary enquiries, um, gen yourself up, gen yourself up on the wider area, and get a sort of heads up on where this is sitting

6B. CAPTURING THE PASSION

ROGER: Okay? *(He throws ball to BRIAN.)* So what position are you in?

BRIAN: *(Dropping the ball.)* I've realized that there's no point trying to make myself passionate about football because I'm never going to be. So what I have to do is I have to forget all that about trying to make myself passionate about football because I'm never going to be. *(Pause.)* Did you get that?

ROGER: Oh for Christ's sake, Brian. We've got Sir Alex Ferguson coming in, and you're saying you can't get passionate about a sport that is the key to us capturing the nation's spirit

BRIAN: I can't –

ROGER: And I'm saying that's ok

BRIAN: Oh, it *is* ok?

ROGER: And I need you now to say 'that's ok but I *will* understand how *other* people *can* become passionate about it.' Can you say that please?

Pause.

BRIAN: No.

Pause.

ROGER: You can't understand why five hundred million people are passionate about football?

BRIAN: Look, we ordered numerous box sets from Amazon of Fergie's 2000 goals, for example. I've watched over and over again, trying to understand why people get passionate about it. And actually there was a sequence of Van... Van... Nestle – roy

ROGER: Ruud Van Nistelrooy. Nistelrooy, yeah. Ruud van Nistelrooy

BRIAN: Nestleroy? Um, and wow I thought, it's pretty good, like an animal, goal after goal after goal. But I think it was just the way they edited the film, because I've tried watching real matches and it's not like that at all. You have to wait for an hour and then there might be a goal. Sorry, what were you talking about?

ROGER: Brian, the passion is not about kicking the ball into the back of the net

BRIAN: What's it about?

ROGER: It's about aligning yourself with –

BRIAN: – with a team

ROGER: – a tribe. It's more than a team, it's a tribe. You've got to see how out there people have nothing going on in their lives, they work at boring jobs, they've got mortgages they won't pay off in their lifetime

BRIAN: Like me

ROGER: They live in places where they weren't brought up, they're lost, uprooted – their life is miserable. But they put on that shirt, and the scarf and the face paint and they go to that stadium, or they go to the pub and they feel that they have a community. That's the passion we're trying to capture, and turn into a British passion. Yes we get it for England matches, or the Scotch get it for the Scottish matches, or the Welsh get it for the Welsh matches, but can we get it for Britain? It hasn't happened.

BRIAN: *(Moving towards ROGER.)* Why don't they just invent some sort of club, people just go, in groups, dressed in their whatever they dress, sing stupid songs for a couple of hours, talk a lot, drink a lot of bollocks and then go home

ROGER: Well that's what football does.

BRIAN: But without all this money involved, I mean

ROGER: What's the problem with the money?

Pause.

ROGER: There's no problem with the money. What's the problem with the money? We stand to make millions out of this for Team GB. The British Olympic Association, the government is going to mint it, big time, selling the rights to watch these games

BRIAN: *We* stand to make money? You and I? Do we?

ROGER: Well *(Coming forward to BRIAN.)* – Pubs, hotels, off licences, they all make money – you might get a pay rise.

BRIAN: A pay rise?

ROGER: Performance related pay and so on – you could become a grade 7

BRIAN: A grade 7? *(BRIAN picks up ball and knees it into his own face.)* Um well in that case I *do* understand why people get passionate about it. I fully understand.

ROGER: This isn't a joke Brian. We've got to get this married up – core values and football. Are you happy?

BRIAN: Um.

ROGER: Let me put it in a different way. Are you very happy, quite happy, not very happy, or not at all happy?

BRIAN: Er

ROGER: I think you're unhappy. But the question is, are you unhappy about it? That's what I want you to find out.

False exit 1.

BRIAN: Well I can tell you now, actually, I mean I've always been what you'd call a bit of a worrier I suppose and what with one thing and another, I mean just lately, what with my apparent infertility, not that I want to tell you about that…

ROGER: Not you, Brian. I don't care about you. It's the British people. Are they happy and if not can we make them happy? Focus on that. Not on GDP but on GWB.

False exit 2.

BRIAN: Get Well Britain?

ROGER: General Well Being. Happiness. Football. Talk to people, get a heads up on it – do a Facebook, Tweet, ask people, ask anyone

Exit upstage – ROGER becomes MIGGY.

7. MIGGY'S BUNGEE BALL

BRIAN: Are you happy, Miggy?

MIGGY: Yes I'm happy, I'm very happy, I'm really happy – really, really happy

BRIAN: Good, that's that covered. I won't ask you why right now. The second thing is do you know anything about football?

BRIAN throws the ball to MIGGY who chests it down, traps it, donkey flicks it up then attaches the bungee rope to it.

MIGGY: I know a bit about football. I play football. Do you play it?

BRIAN: Yes. I was a left back at school.

MIGGY: Left back in the changing rooms *(Laugh.)*. And eh, Bri Bri Bri! Did they pull you off at half time? *(Laugh.)*. As the coach said to the player: Ah, Brian, I think I'm going to have to pull you off at half time. And you said to the coach: Oh can't I just have an orange like everyone else? *(Laughs then gets out a banana.)* It's in my big book – I have to learn all this for my citizenshit test – and the national anthem, some poems, the poems are beautiful – 'I want to go to the seaside, I want to go to the sea' *(To the tune of Glory, glory, hallelujiah.)* from the heart; Winston Churchill speaking its good. Do you want a go with the bungee? It looks good. You can tell to your kids

Pause.

MIGGY: My five, they love it, the tricks with the bungee, *(Peels banana, throws fruit, keeps skin, laughs, throws skin.)* even the little one – he's three – he has a go on the pitch then we have a match against our upstairs neighbor – Chinese – there are 6 of them, China v Algeria world cup final – it's a good match. You can be Britain.

BRIAN: Alright *(Starts putting the elastic ball on.).*

MIGGY launches into a loud rendition of Rule Britannia.

BRIAN: Miggy, Miggy, Miggy, We're in Britain, all right? We don't raise our voices here. It's not done.

MIGGY: Come on, take the beanpole out of your bottom

BRIAN: What?

MIGGY: Take the broom handle out of your ass – huh – 'If I should die think only this of me….' You know that one?

BRIAN: Oh yes. There is some corner of a foreign field that is forever England. There shall be in that rich earth…

MIGGY: Or Sir Smashem Up. Yeah?

BRIAN: Oh, Good afternoon, Sir Smashem up. We're having tea, do take a cup. sugar and milk? Now let me see? Two lumps, I think. Good gracious me. The silly thing slipped off your knee. Pray don't apologize old chap. A very trivial mishap. We've got at least a dozen more. Just leave the pieces on the floor

MIGGY: Come and live with me and be my love....

BRIAN: Oh yes. And we will all the pleasures prove that hills and valleys, dales and fields and all the craggy mountains yields. Let us sit upon the rocks and see the shepherds feed their flocks by something rivers upon whose falls melodious birds sing madrigals. And I will give thee beds of roses, made with a thousand fragrant poses. And if these pleasures should thee move, come live with me...

MIGGY encourages him – from the heart, etc... takes off his overalls. MIGGY has become ROGER with fresh towel rolled up under arm ready for squash match, to whom BRIAN now delivers the final line of verse.

BRIAN: And be my love.

8A. THE CORE BRITISH VALUES

ROGER wiggles his pelvis – apparently with excitement at this proposition but actually warming up for squash – which he continues to do through this exchange with his towel rolled up under his arm.

ROGER: Got to the bottom of Britishness for me?

BRIAN: I'm getting to the bottom of it

ROGER: What would you say are the five core British values Brian?

BRIAN: Well tolerance, decency, patience and stiff upper lip.

ROGER: That's four isn't it?

BRIAN: Those are the ... the basic values.

ROGER: How do they relate to the cardinal virtues?

BRIAN: What are the cardinal virtues?

ROGER: I'm not sure, but prudence ... courage, and ... what did you say your four were? Stiff upper lip?

BRIAN: Tolerance.

ROGER: Yes, stiff upper lip and tolerance … there's another one. Aren't stiff upper lip and tolerance sort of the same thing?

BRIAN: Ah, no.

ROGER: What's the difference?

BRIAN: It's a different class or levels like cause of its … tolerance is, is, tolerate, tolerating your fellow man.

ROGER: Right.

BRIAN: Stiff upper lip is being able to put up with things.

ROGER: So, tolerance is putting up with your fellow man and stiff upper lip is putting up with things. I don't see the difference there. I, I think we need a bit more clarity, yeah? For the Mrs Singh in the street, if she's to have concrete concepts that she can align herself with so that when she sees a coffin draped in a Union Jack of a soldier killed on the Pakistan border – her country – she has tears in her eyes. I want you to get three people off the street

BRIAN: Real members of the public?

ROGER: Yes

BRIAN: Literally off the street?

ROGER: Literally off the street

BRIAN: I can go and get them now?

ROGER: If you need to, yeah. Bring them in

BRIAN: Alright.

8B. THE FOCUS GROUP

ROGER: *(Towel now around neck – post workout.)* So who have we got?

BRIAN: Well, him, him and him.

Non-blinding lights on separate seats in auditorium.

ROGER: And who are they?

BRIAN: Sorry, and her.

Another light comes on a person in the auditorium.

ROGER: They are all white folk?

BRIAN: Yes, yes, yes, yes.

ROGER: And you represent Britain, ok?

BRIAN: Yes, they represent Britain.

ROGER: Ok – so try and get a heads up on what you think are the greatest cultural sporting, sporting cultural, historical sporting, historical cultural sporting moments in British history. Could you do that by lunch?

8C. SPINE TINGLERS

ROGER: So what have we got?

BRIAN: The Iraq war.

ROGER: What about something sporting – something spine-tingling?

BRIAN: There's the Beckham penalty against Argentina. I was there, actually, when it happened. I was in Japan, I was in Tokyo in 2002. I picked up a fungal toenail infection.

ROGER: So…something spine-tingling? I recently had a spine-tingling moment watching the video of the IOC meeting in Singapore. When Jaques Rogge revealed the bid winner using all the techniques of a Big Brother eviction announcement

BRIAN: Oh right. Yes, it's one of those moments where everyone knows where they were when it happened.

ROGER: The very last word was the name of the winning city. Something like 'I am very pleased to announce…the winner…of…

BRIAN: He was Chinese?

ROGER: ...the winner...of...the competition ... to hold the one hundred twenty seven Olympiad...

BRIAN: Was this intentional or was it just because his command of English was not very good?

ROGER: Oh I'm absolutely sure it was intentional

BRIAN: Oh right. Scripted.

ROGER: Yeah

BRIAN: Probably rehearsed

ROGER: Yes '...in twenty twelve...is...the city...of... London!' And then the London delegates went crazy. And then I got the spine-tingly moment.

BRIAN: *You* got the spine-tingling moment?

ROGER: I did. Even watching it on youtube... It was incredible

BRIAN: Jesus.

ROGER: Anyway, that's what we're looking for. That's why we've got the focus group. So, ok, Guys. Everybody clear about what they need to do?

BRIAN moves downstage as if to approach the audience.

ROGER: *(Just to BRIAN.)* Has Sir Alex arrived yet?

BRIAN: Yes, he's here

BRIAN takes a football boot that's hidden under the front rostra and stashes ROGER's used towel.

9 SIR ALEX

ROGER: Sir Alex, um...you were going to say at our last meeting how you're planning to beat the Brazilians and the Argentinians

SIR ALEX: *(Pacing back and forth.)* Beat the Brazilians and the Argies?

ROGER: With the age restriction that is imposed on the Olympic football events of twenty-three-years-old meaning that most of our sort of golden age marquee players are not within that age range whereas we know the Brazilians and the Argentinians have bizillions of Brazilians who are under the age and therefore capable of sweeping the competition with their brilliance? How to stamp that out? Is it a climate thing? Should we schedule the matches in the rain? In Scotland? What's your thinking?

SIR ALEX: Um…well I thought I might retire. Actually I'm getting a bit old.

ROGER: From Manchester United?

SIR ALEX: Aye. I mean after the recent failures I'm thinking maybe I've had enough.

ROGER: So what are you saying? You're not going to manage Team GB?

SIR ALEX: *(Stopping in front of ROGER to say this.)* Well I'm not sure. I'm having second thoughts about it. It's a big job, you know.

ROGER: I do know that and I thought this would be the crowning glory of your career.

SFX : Phone rings

ROGER: Sorry, I'd better take this. *(He goes upstage.)* Jeffreys. Aha, I understand, right. Ok, I'll tell him. Mm.

Looks at phone in disbelief then slumps down in chair.

SIR ALEX: Mm?

ROGER: *(To A.)* The um Scottish football association, the Welsh FA and Football Northern Ireland have come to an agreement with FIFA and they're not going to allow their players to be part of the team. But they're willing to allow only English players to represent Britain.

SIR ALEX: Well then it's not Britain, is it?

ROGER: Well no it… they don't want to compromise their…
I think it's actually rather a good outcome, it's not the
outcome we officially wanted but –

SIR ALEX: We can't call it Team GB then, can we?

ROGER: Well, we're going to have to. It is Team GB.

SIR ALEX: It's English. English team.

*He throws the football boot at ROGER, who ducks. The boot hits the
wall and ROGER picks it up.*

ROGER: There won't be any Scottish, Welsh or Irish players –
which there probably won't be anyway – How do you feel
about that?

SIR ALEX: I don't feel right about it.

ROGER: So who do you think we should have in the squad?

SIR ALEX: Not good at all.

ROGER: Under twenty-three and English. Who are we going
to have? Anyone you want. Any English player you want.
Bearing in mind now this is in two years' time. *(Pause.)*
Three years' time. *(Pause.)* Three years from now, so –

SIR ALEX: *(Boiling with rage.)* I canna remember their names.
Forgotten. Me memory's not as good as it used to be.
That's another reason I was thinking maybe I should get
out now.

ROGER retreats and gets the high status chair to hide behind.

10. THE TEAM LIST

ROGER brings up the high status chair behind BRIAN so that he sits in it.

ROGER: Brian, it didn't go great with Sir Alex –

BRIAN: Oh I'm sorry to hear that. Why not?

ROGER: It's not looking very good is it?

BRIAN: For my pay rise, you mean?

ROGER: Have we got anybody else lined up? What about Fabio Capello?

BRIAN: I do actually need that pay rise. Quite badly in fact.

ROGER: And er could we make some recommendations about the under twenty-three players – Aaron Lennon, for example. Any others that come to mind? –

BRIAN: Um…

ROGER: Could you perhaps scribble up a list of –

BRIAN: Me?

ROGER: – under twenty-three English –

BRIAN: I can. Not now but yes, I will –

ROGER: – premiership players. Get back to me with that quickly

BRIAN: Yes ok…

ROGER: *(Bringing up chair behind BRIAN again and causing him to sit again.)* So how's the list?

BRIAN: …in a few days

ROGER: Who's on it?

BRIAN: What? Now?

ROGER: Yes. Who's on it?

BRIAN: What?

ROGER: Who's on it?

BRIAN: No. Steady on.

ROGER: You've had three days.

BRIAN: Not – yes, it's not long enough. Been busy.

ROGER: Ok, well how long do you need?

BRIAN: Well, a few months

ROGER: Ok. I'll see you in a few months.

BRIAN: Alright.

> *BRIAN rises and steps forward.*

> *ROGER brings up chair behind BRIAN.*

ROGER: Ok so Brian how did it go?

BRIAN: Steady on. Well I've been busy.

ROGER: The Olympics –

BRIAN: Look, come on.

ROGER: – are in eighteen –

BRIAN: *(He consults folder that's in back of the chair.)* Alright –

ROGER: – months time –

BRIAN: No. It's four years away.

ROGER: I'll have moved on by then. They've got me in mind for the DTI. We're on 18 month portfolios

BRIAN: Alright

ROGER: You haven't done your work, have you, Brian?

> *Raising shoe above head in the style of SIR ALEX earlier and addressing the audience through this next section as if other players in a dressing room dressing down speech, humiliating BRIAN in front of them.*

BRIAN: *(Finding the answers aren't in the folder.)* Alright. Brian McGovern –

ROGER: Ok, Brian McGovern.

BRIAN: Yes, Frank –

ROGER: He's Scottish. He's over twenty –

BRIAN: Frank Peters

ROGER: He's English, he's…he's probably dead. Go on.

BRIAN: What do you mean?

ROGER: Frank Peters? How old is Frank –

BRIAN: I made him up. What are you talking about? Is there one called Frank Peters?

ROGER: Yeah he's a –

BRIAN: You're kidding

ROGER: He's an old –

BRIAN: You're joking

ROGER: No he's an old…no, it's *Martin* Peters. Sorry. It's Martin Peters, a famous –

BRIAN: Ok

ROGER: – a famous Leeds United player. You're probably mixing him up with Frank Lampard

BRIAN: I just made it up –

ROGER: 'I just made it up'? You haven't read the new guidelines have you Brian?

BRIAN: Yes, I know, all of us in the department have got to try and change the way we speak and I have been trying.

ROGER: It's not just changing the way, Brian. You've got to connect with the public, we've all got to, with the man in the street, and the way to connect with them is to speak like them, or like most of them, you know, which is Estuarine English. Come on do it!

Pause.

I might have to pull you off.

BRIAN: *(In estuarine English accent.)* Michael McMahon

ROGER laughs.

BRIAN: What?

ROGER: He's English? Is he English?

BRIAN: Yes.

ROGER: Have you asked –

BRIAN: Yes he's English, yes he is

ROGER: You're sure he hasn't become an Australian? …
Who's he signed with? Are they prepared to release him?

BRIAN: Bromley.

ROGER laughs.

ROGER: Bromley?

BRIAN: I don't know

ROGER: They're in the Confed

BRIAN: Oh sorry. Um –

ROGER: We need premiership players under the age of
twenty-three, for fuck's sake, Brian

*ROGER throws boot at back wall trying to emulate SIR ALEX but
coming off a bit ineffectually*

BRIAN: Alright, sorry. Um…oh gosh, hang on. There is um…

ROGER: Let me tell you about something else –

BRIAN: Ah. Martin Bell.

ROGER: Martin Bell. That's a brand of…dairy products.

BRIAN: That's Baby Bell.

ROGER: No, come on, I want to tell you about something else,
I want to talk to you about something else.

BRIAN: Yes, go on

ROGER: Now –

BRIAN: Personal?

ROGER: No, no, no, it's to do with the team

BRIAN: Right.

ROGER: I need you to think of a spokesperson or ambassador
– perhaps an iconic sporting figure – not too expensive –
that can lead this 'Celebration of Britain' seminar series

for us – as obviously you're not going to be able to *(Slaps BRIAN's papers/folder.)*

BRIAN: Me?

ROGER: and don't say Usain Bolt.

BRIAN: Pardon?

ROGER: Don't say Usain Bolt. He's no use to us

BRIAN: Ah

ROGER: He's no use to us.

BRIAN: Mm, mm. Um…

Pause.

ROGER: Brian, you know who Usain Bolt is?

BRIAN: No.

ROGER: Don't you?

BRIAN: Who?

ROGER: Usain Bolt.

BRIAN: No.

ROGER laughs.

BRIAN: What?

ROGER: Who do you think Usain Bolt is?

BRIAN: I haven't a clue

ROGER: Come on, have a wild guess.

BRIAN: Is it an anagram?

ROGER laughs.

BRIAN: Let me have a look at this.

BRIAN takes a pen from his pocket, gets up and takes some paper from a pile downstage left. During the following he spreads out the pages, each with a letter on, and begins to form a football pitch corner shape out of them.

BRIAN: Usain –

ROGER: Usain Bolt. I'll spell it for you.

BRIAN: Yes, I think it's an anagram.

ROGER: U-S-A-I-N. New word, B-O-L-T.

BRIAN mumbles some possible solutions– Anus Boil, soil bun etc...

ROGER: No? Doesn't ring any bells? Does it ring any bells? Usain Bolt. Anything?

BRIAN: Are you trying to be funny?

ROGER: No I'm not trying to be funny. That's a person's name, ok? It's related to a magical sporting moment or two or twenty. Um…

BRIAN: Oh ok.

ROGER: Do anything for you? You haven't got a clue who that is, have you?

BRIAN: Why should I?

ROGER: You're working for the fucking –

BRIAN: Is he a footballer?

ROGER: British –

BRIAN: Footballer?

ROGER: No. You're working for the British Olympic Committee –

BRIAN: It sounds like a –

ROGER: On the London 2012 Olympics –

BRIAN: Sorry, it sounds like – it's a fiction

ROGER: And you don't even know –

BRIAN: This is a trick question, I know. Come on. Usain Bolt my arse.

ROGER: For fuck's sake

BRIAN: Usain Bolt.

ROGER: Brian, we – we –

BRIAN: Come on.

ROGER: We organized the 150-metre –

BRIAN: Oh! Usain Bolt. Sorry, sorry, I thought you were pulling my leg

ROGER: Oh it was my accent, was it?

BRIAN: Yes, yes, yes, yes, yes, yes, great guy.

ROGER: Mm, mm.

BRIAN: …It is a man, isn't it?

11A. NIGEL SNIFFING

BRIAN stands in the corner.

NIGEL: Was that Roger Jeffries you were talking to?

BRIAN: Yes. Yes.

NIGEL: What was he after?

BRIAN: You haven't met him before, Nigel?

NIGEL: Was it to do with this new directive that's supposed to be coming out?

BRIAN: Which new directive?

NIGEL: About team GB? *(Seeing a piece of paper with that written on it and picking it up.)*

BRIAN: I don't know anything about it

NIGEL: Well if you wanna do any preparation in the event of us having to get something together.

BRIAN: No it's, it's. Well. Actually, no it's fine.

NIGEL: Right.

BRIAN: Anyway, thanks for the offer.

NIGEL: I've finished up. You know, the stuff on disabilities. So, yeah, whenever you're ready…

He has sat down in the high status chair and put his feet up on the middle ranking one and scrumpled up the Team GB paper into a ball.

BRIAN: Oh yeah yeah yeah.

NIGEL: I've kind of drawn the line under that one.

BRIAN: *(coming out of his corner.)* You're not a football fan, are you?

NIGEL: Oh yeah. Yeah, I follow the Arsenal. I'm a season ticket holder

BRIAN: Oh right. Me too.

NIGEL: Oh are you?

BRIAN: Well, not the Arsenal. Some other team.

NIGEL: *(He lines up BRIAN.)* So who do you follow?

BRIAN: Ah, Everton.

NIGEL: *(He jumps his chair forward towards BRIAN.)* The toffees?

BRIAN: Yeah yeah yeah. The toffees.

NIGEL: How did you get into them?

BRIAN: Oh, I had an uncle from round there. But – yes *(Trying to change the subject.)* be interesting to have your thoughts

NIGEL: On football?

11B NUTMEG

BRIAN: Do you know what a nutmeg is?

NIGEL: Yeah – It's like a lollipop – Do you know what a lollipop is?

BRIAN: A sweet thing you lick

NIGEL: This is the ball, right. *(He lobs the scrunched up ball of paper onto the floor.)* That's you, you're the black player

He places the high status chair he was sitting on near the ball

BRIAN: Black?

NIGEL: Yeah

BRIAN: Shouldn't we make it race neutral?

NIGEL: Okay you're the blue player

He pushes the high status black chair downstage and grabs the middle ranking blue chair placing it behind the ball.

BRIAN: Right

NIGEL: I'm the black player, *(He gets behind the high status chair.)* I've got the ball, this is the lollipop yeah – you're coming to attack – you're coming to attack, like that, I knock the ball past you *(Throws the paper ball to one side of the blue chair.)* – And as you're thinking 'where's it gone?' turning *(He manipulates blue chair – swiveling it on the spot.)* – I sprint past here, collect the ball and carry on

He pushes the black chair past the blue one picks up the paper ball and sits down in the black chair.

BRIAN: And what's that called?

NIGEL: That's called The Lollipop. Now, The Nutmeg.

BRIAN: Yes

NIGEL: ...is through the legs like that. *(Gets up throws paper ball under the chair, picks it up and sits down again in the black chair, picking up the shoe that ROGER threw at the same time.)* As opposed to around the side – it's considered to be the ultimate insult to an opponent – but the whole point with these skills

BRIAN: *(Moving downstage as something begins to dawn on him.)* It's psychological, isn't it? You end up feeling a twat. Which we will anyway, won't we, when we lose.

NIGEL: Eh? Yeah you fire them up then you've got to deal with that

BRIAN: They get angry?

NIGEL: Yeah. They get fucking angry *(He slaps his chair with the shoe as if riding a horse.)* and then they outplay you.

11 C BECKHAM 98

BRIAN: Well they will get angry, won't they, when we lose. Why don't we just get what's his name, you know, the pug-faced guy?

NIGEL: Rooney?

BRIAN: Yes, why don't we get the Rooney-faced pug guy sent off? So we lose for other reasons.

NIGEL: Like escapegoat him ?

BRIAN: Yes. If it looks like we're gonna lose let's fuck it up.

NIGEL: A Beckham '98?

BRIAN: What's that?

NIGEL: A Beckham '98?

He gets up strikes both chairs, the shoe and scrumpled ball.

BRIAN: Where he refused to shake hands with err. With umm...

NIGEL: No where he kicked back at

BRIAN: Simeoni

NIGEL: I'll show you *(Stands.)*. Simeoni's just fouled him, right. Bang. He's on the ground.

BRIAN: Simeoni?

NIGEL: No

BRIAN: Do you want me to be Simeoni?

NIGEL: Yeah go on

BRIAN: or I should be Beckham?

NIGEL gets on floor.

BRIAN: Who are you?

NIGEL: Simeoni's just walking back having fouled me

BRIAN: Who are you?

NIGEL: I'm Beckham

BRIAN: *(Walks across front of stage SL to SR.)* I'm like this? Walking back?

NIGEL: Walk this way *(Illustrates with his hand.)*

BRIAN: *(Gets in DSL position but doesn't move just clarifies what he's meant to do.)* Walk towards you?

NIGEL: Yeah

BRIAN: *(Clarifying further.)* Walk away?

NIGEL: Backwards towards me

BRIAN walks backwards to NIGEL.

NIGEL: Closer, closer, Miroslav Klose

NIGEL Kicks him, BRIAN falls in agony.

NIGEL: Yeah, you got it, yeah. And make a big thing out of it.

BRIAN turns it into big dramatic death scene.

NIGEL: *(Encourages.)* ...Keep going, yeah yeah milk it milk it

He does but it could just as easily be him producing a sperm sample for the IVF clinic.

12. SOME FIGURES

NIGEL becomes ROGER wielding a yellow notebook/diary rather like a yellow card.

ROGER: What are you doing Brian?

BRIAN stays on the floor.

BRIAN: I've been watching football

ROGER: Yes.

BRIAN: I've been watching it, trying to get into it and trying to feel the passion that other people feel for this beautiful game.

ROGER: During work hours or after work hours?

BRIAN: Mostly after work hours.

ROGER: That's very commendable. You know obviously we won't be paying you any overtime for that

BRIAN: No, I know that

ROGER: I appreciate the effort.

BRIAN: That's all right

ROGER: I appreciate your discretion in, in this matter. So you're trying to understand the passion that people feel for the sport?

BRIAN: Yes, well obviously quite a lot of people find it very interesting, this game…

ROGER: Five hundred million.

BRIAN: It's trying to identify with, with that and find out what, what drives these people to go to these stadiums and watch…

ROGER: Men kicking a bag of air around?

BRIAN: Exactly.

ROGER: And what conclusions have you come to? Because we need to sign off on this urgently

BRIAN: Well so far I haven't really connected with it myself I have to say.

ROGER: That's all right, that's all right.

BRIAN: Well it doesn't have to be, but you know it probably takes a while. Um, sorry, what was the question?

ROGER: Get me some numbers – People who do align themselves with football games, of the 57 million, and

happiness, general well-being as related to sport and
cultural activity

*BRIAN hobbles over on his knees to the piles of paper downstage left
and pulls them up and lays them down during following. First a
line before the front row of the audience, then a semi-circle corner
line, then a line along stage left and a penalty spot upstage right-ish.*

*ROGER wants to leave but reluctantly lingers to hear BRIAN out –
dropping in and out of the room and other problems occasionally
throwing in a 'right', 'interesting', 'good', 'okay', etc.*

BRIAN: Yes, well I've now had the completed questionnaires
handed back from 30,000 Premier League Club supporters
and another 30,000 from what we call the man in the street
and basically the statistics are showing us that ticket prices
have escalated to exorbitant levels, season ticket holders
are getting richer as well as happier while the man in the
street is not very happy at all though generally thinks that
he would be able to find happiness through participation
in a sporting activity, specifically as a spectator of that
activity and even more specifically when his own country
is seen to be winning at that activity. I do have further
statistics as well and models of course in other countries,
though I'm not suggesting we should follow these, where
the happiness, or GWB as we're calling it, *(No interjections
from ROGER temporarily.)* of its citizens is a priority, for
example, the tiny Himalayan state of Bhutan – is that
how you pronounce it? Or should it be Bhutan with the
emphasis on the 'Bhu' – oh you're not listening, are you,
anyway, so I'm going to take this opportunity to reflect
further on my private life and my upcoming problems, and
the fact that I'm deeply unhappy at the prospect of this
bloody sperm donor, when he comes, if he comes, sorry,
no pun intended. And is happiness to be located anyway
in making additions to an already over-crowded world,
even though of course it's not technically me who's doing
the adding, I suppose, is it? But actually, Bhutan – with the
emphasis on the 'tan' this time – measures its economic
development and growth not with the conventional

measure of GDP but with the holistic, multidimensional measure of Gross National Happiness, *(ROGER in view but on telephone off stage.)* which is based on economic self-reliance, environmental preservation, cultural promotion, which includes sport, of course, and good governance as well. A fact which I can see is boring the pants off you, if indeed you're listening at all, are you, bollocks, shit, pompous git, pee on my grandmother's face, no you're not. But as far as the topic of Britishness applied to sport is concerned, I discovered there's a lot of Britishness around but …. not as applied to sport. That's a new thing, that's a document we're going to have to create isn't it, a codification of British values as embodied in sport. Because sport, as you know, is this country's international shop window, and when I was working on the Britishness questionnaire for immigrants that sort of thing cropped up frequently. and 'Who is the Prime Minister?' was another, 'what's the name of the Prime Minister?'

ROGER: Yes, what is the name of the Prime Minister?

BRIAN: Which interestingly actually is also one of the tests for um, for what's the word? Insipid? Insipient Alzheimer's, it's one of the test questions there. Um, Dame Iris Murdoch, there's a film with her being interviewed and they ask her who is the British Prime Minister and she doesn't know, sorry that's a bit… And also they say to her: Have you written any, any books as yet and… I don't know. Sorry, you see my interests lie elsewhere

BRIAN stands up.

ROGER: Yes, you're obviously an arty-farty, more culture side of …

BRIAN: Well that's how I, how I came into it, you know …

ROGER: How are you getting on with the actual game of football, the actual rules of actual football?

BRIAN: Oh I think I understand the game, I understand the rules of the game as far as…

ROGER: What I've always wanted to know, Brian, is what this bloody offside rule is all about. Can you explain it to me?

BRIAN: Oh yes well it's um basically when somebody's not on the side, you know, which means they're off the side, isn't it? Something like that.

He demonstrates by jumping over the side line stage left. He giggles. A deathly pause.

ROGER: This isn't a joke, you know. We're all on the line here. My career is hanging on this, and yours.

BRIAN: On the offside rule?

ROGER: And if you can't explain it then I'm going to have to find somebody who can.

BRIAN: Oh no, well I understand, Sir Roger, I understand all the rules of the game.

ROGER: Put them in a nutshell for me?

BRIAN: Well, you know, don't you?

ROGER: I'm just the… I'm devil's advocate, I don't know anything about football… *(Hands in the air he sits in the front row of the auditorium.)*

BRIAN: Oh right …

ROGER: I'm Mrs Rajiv Singh from Leicester,

BRIAN: Yes,

ROGER: Ah, I need to be persuaded to align myself with Britishness through football, what's this game, football?

BRIAN: Well it's a game where you, you have, you have two teams, um, I've forgotten, how many on a team? I've forgotten. Twelve is it?

ROGER: *(Indian accent.)* I don't know what it is.

BRIAN: Something like twelve anyway and, some number like that, each team. Basically you've got twenty-two millionaires ruining a lawn. *(He goes to edge, stage left, as though to bring on some chairs, but hesitates and stands still instead.)* And um…actually this is when I'm beginning to regret I haven't done the research.

13 NIGEL'S BREAKFAST

ROGER becomes NIGEL carrying a large take-away coffee (Grande Venti Latte) and a shiny Jabulani football. He is in a foul mood because last night Everton (supposedly BRIAN's team) beat his team – Arsenal.

NIGEL: Trying out some new office arrangements?

BRIAN: There was going to be a seminar. It's actually been cancelled now.

NIGEL: What's the topic?

BRIAN: Oh it was on…I've forgotten.

NIGEL: A celebration of Britain?

BRIAN: Yeah

NIGEL: Isn't that a bit offensive? *(Bounces ball.)*

BRIAN: What?

NIGEL: People will think it's a bit BNP ish isn't it?

Bounces ball then rolls it onto the ground and does a lollipop around BRIAN from USL to DSR.

BRIAN: No… Patriotism is a love of country that's all – its gives you a sense of security and belonging. It makes you complete and happy. Like me

NIGEL: Well I wanna do that

BRIAN: Do you?

NIGEL: Yeah. Let's have a celebration – Let's all have a disco nan na na na na na na na – What can we celebrate about Britain today? *(Throws ball to BRIAN.)*

BRIAN: *(Throwing ball back at NIGEL.)* Well I can throw that back at you. What can we celebrate about Britain today, Nigel?

NIGEL: Well…

Arranges ball on top of coffee cup, addressing it as Yorick's skull/ the world etc.

BRIAN: Where are you from?

NIGEL: *(Not thinking.)* I'm from Bebington.

BRIAN: Oh yeah, Bebington. I know it.

NIGEL: *(Not thinking.)* Yeah?

BRIAN: The Wirral – no?

NIGEL: *(This is what he's been thinking about.)* It's about the core British values, isn't it? It's about keeping this island believing in what it is.

BRIAN: *(Moving towards him.)* Ah hang on, can you say that last sentence again please?

NIGEL: keeping this island believing in what it is?

BRIAN: *(Mimicking him.)* 'keeping this island believing in what it is'

NIGEL: Are you taking the piss?

BRIAN: *(Still mimicking.)* 'You taking the piss?'

NIGEL: You're taking the piss, aren't you?

NIGEL shoves BRIAN – right hand to right shoulder. BRIAN pushes him back – right hand to NIGEL's left shoulder. The latte is spilled and the ball rolls off to stage right – NIGEL has been facing upstage.

NIGEL: You've made me spill my breakfast all over the place. You better clean that up Bri – that's health and safety that is

BRIAN: I'll get a mop

NIGEL: I'll have to get Miggy the Argie– cos this is a health and safety issue here – we can't work in this area

NIGEL becomes MIGGY.

14. BRIAN GIVES MIGGY THE CITIZENSHIP TEST

BRIAN: Miguel, Nigel made a mess of his breakfast. He got carried away. Clean it up.

MIGGY: *(As he cleans the mess up on his knees with a sponge he recites from his red notebook.)* I must go down to the sea again, the lonely sea and sky. I left me shoes and socks there, I wonder if they're dry

He puts his red notebook in his breast pocket

BRIAN: How long have you been in this country, Miggy?

MIGGY: Three years

BRIAN: Are you on a work permit, or what?

MIGGY: Yeah

BRIAN: How long does that last?

MIGGY: Five years

BRIAN: What are you going to do then when it expires? You're going to apply for another one, are you?

MIGGY: I've applied for British citizen. Do the test. Do the test. I'll be a loyal British subject.

BRIAN: Alright then. So here's your first citizenship question.

MIGGY: Hit me, hit me with it

BRIAN: If you saw a troop carrying a Union Jack, how would you feel?

MIGGY: What? What's a troop?

BRIAN: Army.

MIGGY: Troop? Oh no no no. Don't like. Don't like fighting, no. Disgusting, we don't want to fight.

BRIAN: That's the wrong answer.

MIGGY: Say it again, say it again.

BRIAN: If you see a British army troop carrying a coffin, all right?

MIGGY: Coffin?

BRIAN: With a Union Jack over it

MIGGY: Oh Union Jack is good.

BRIAN: How do you feel about that?

MIGGY: Union Jack. Yes. Great.

BRIAN: Oh. You see the Union Jack and you feel great?

MIGGY: Coffin not. Coffin is bad stuff.

BRIAN: So how do you feel?

MIGGY: I feel like patriotic.

BRIAN: Yes?

MIGGY: Mm.

BRIAN: Does it bring tears to your eyes?

MIGGY: No. Never.

BRIAN: That's the wrong answer. You'll have to get married, Miggy. You'll have to marry some 'large' *(Consciously mocking pc.)* person with self-esteem issues

MIGGY: A Brit?

BRIAN: Yes.

MIGGY: I got wife already

BRIAN: How many wives can you have in your religion? Whatever your religion is. What is your religion?

MIGGY: I'm Catholic

BRIAN: How many wives you allowed in Catholicism?

MIGGY: Only the one. Only the one they know about

BRIAN: So you could have another one and then just confess to the pedophile in the box and then everything would be all right?

MIGGY: No it would not be all right. It wouldn't be acknowledged in the eyes of God and the church, you see

BRIAN: So you have to annul the first one?

MIGGY: You couldn't even do it

BRIAN: Why couldn't you annul the first one?

MIGGY: No you couldn't have two wives. Impossible

BRIAN: Why can't you say 'we've grown apart'? So the marriage has become insolvent.

MIGGY: I love my wife

BRIAN: *(Ignoring him.)* Yes. Why don't you say that? And then get yourself some woman who's desperate. Here's your next citizenship question. What are the five core British values?

MIGGY: Marks and Spenser's? Tesco…

BRIAN: Wrong answer – Which cricket team do you support?

MIGGY: Oh yes West Indies

BRIAN: What?

MIGGY: West Indies

BRIAN: Wrong answer

MIGGY: Why? I'm supposed to support who? West Sussex?

BRIAN: You're supposed to support England. Say England is playing Argentina, your country.

MIGGY: I'm from Algeria

BRIAN: Well, they're against England, aren't they? Who would you want to win that game?

MIGGY: Well I want to watch beautiful football. I just want to see the Dutch passing, the Italian defence

BRIAN: Who do you want to win?

MIGGY: The Germans' application, beautiful, sexy –

BRIAN: England versus Argentina. The Argies are leading two-nil they score – it's three-nil – to Argentina – How do you feel about that? Do you feel good about that? *(MIGGY hides behind his poetry book.)* Are you smiling Miggy? *(MIGGY lowers book to prove he's not smiling.)* Okay, it's five-nil, five-nil to Argentina, *(MIGGY hides behind his poetry book to smile.)* How do you feel now? Five-nil, how do you feel? How do you feel? *(MIGGY lowers book to prove he's not smiling.)* Eight-nil, *(MIGGY hides behind his poetry book to smile.)* how do you feel now? Feel good yeah? *(MIGGY lowers book to prove he's not smiling.)* Nine-nil *(MIGGY hides behind his poetry book to smile then lowers it to prove he's not smiling.)* Twelve-nil *(MIGGY hides behind his poetry book to smile then lowers it to prove he's not smiling.)* Is that the book for your citizenship test?

MIGGY: It's just my poems – citizenship test – big book

BRIAN: Can I have a look?

MIGGY: Yeah, its nothing, it's not important

BRIAN: Oh so this is Great Britain, is it? Oh, not important, you say?

MIGGY: Yes not that important

BRIAN: You're sure it's not important?

MIGGY: Yes yes sure

BRIAN: It looks like you put a lot of work into it

BRIAN rips up MIGGY's pages.

MIGGY becomes NIGEL.

15A. BRIAN'S VOLUNTARY SUBSTITUTION

NIGEL: Oh dear, this won't look good on your performance report Brian. *(Pause.)* Sir Roger wants to see you in his office

BRIAN: I can't go. I'm going to a donor conception counseling session.

NIGEL: What, you can't…?

BRIAN: No, I can't. I think the size of my balls might have something to do with it.

NIGEL: You've got small balls?

BRIAN: Well I wouldn't…yes. I don't know how I feel about it either, having a donor conceived child, if that's what it's going to come to. I mean I don't know if I'll be able to bond with it. Though I think I will because I have successfully bonded with our cat.

NIGEL: I know where you're coming from, mate. I successfully bonded with our guinea pig, though having said that I came down one morning, patted it on the head, it bit me, keeled over and died.

BRIAN: Sorry.

NIGEL: It's all right. I was only six. *(Laughs.)* But it's cloning, isn't it? Dolly the sheep? Don't you think it's a bit perverse? I saw a picture of a rat once with a human ear growing on its back.

BRIAN: Thanks for your support. You couldn't go instead, could you?

NIGEL: To your cloning session? Give 'em a dollop? Done all that as a student at Ealing Poly – there's a couple of gallons of mine in the freezer at the local.

BRIAN: I meant to the launch of the Celebration of Britain series in Salisbury– it's a low key thing – I don't know if anyone will show up.

NIGEL: Didn't you do that in Dubai?

BRIAN: Yes

NIGEL: How come you get all the good junkets?

BRIAN: I don't know!

NIGEL: Why do I have to go to fucking Salisbury and you get to go to Dubai?

BRIAN: What's wrong with Salisbury?

NIGEL: Oh yeah, its quite good actually

BRIAN: Hanging around with Roger Jeffreys – maybe the next one will be a bit more glamorous

NIGEL: You want me to go to the next one too?

BRIAN: Maybe all of them.. and get the print material ordered? I'm going to pull myself off

NIGEL: At the cloning clinic?

BRIAN: The project. I have to be available at any time. What was it that Roger wanted?

NIGEL: Nothing much. He just wanted someone to fill him in on the offside rule.

BRIAN: Ah, yes well I could have told him that.

NIGEL: Don't worry, mate. It's done. Sorted

BRIAN: And?

Pause.

NIGEL: *(On the verge of tears.)* I suppose you're happy with what the toffees did to Arsenal last night?

BRIAN: Oh, is that what all this is about?

NIGEL: Yeah, and you're happy about it?

BRIAN: Yes.. and the Scousers will be happy *(NIGEL slams the wall.)* – because people from Everton are all Scousers aren't they?

NIGEL: Yeah

BRIAN: Just like people from The Wirral

NIGEL: Yeah

BRIAN: Where Bebington is

NIGEL: Yeah

BRIAN: Where you're from

NIGEL: Yeah I

BRIAN: You don't sound like a Scouser

NIGEL: Well you don't sound like where you're from

BRIAN: Rugby?

NIGEL becomes ROGER.

ROGER: Rugby? You were *at* Rugby?

BRIAN: I was at Rugby proper not Rugby Grammar before …
um … And then I went up to Oxford.

ROGER: Right.

BRIAN: Polytechnic.

ROGER: You were a chancellor?

BRIAN: Yes

ROGER: Are you married, Brian?

BRIAN: Yes.

ROGER: Children?

BRIAN: Well, we've been um….no.

ROGER: Oh good. I was just thinking, Brian, that Nigel, the
EO might be a rather useful asset for us

ROGER takes a wander downstage.

BRIAN: Who? What?

ROGER: Nigel – he could be the acting HEO spokesperson

BRIAN: Sorry. Acting HEO?

ROGER: Yes, the ambassador – spokesperson, for the Celebration of Britain seminars, I like his – authentic. Do you have that document ready yet, Brian?

BRIAN: Eh, no. Not exactly.

ROGER: Could you email it to me?

BRIAN: Yes,

ROGER: Okay well you go off and do that – soon as please, and copy Nigel in so he can start preparing

BRIAN: Shouldn't I be doing it?– I mean I did write it after all

ROGER: Time to pass it on Brian – you've been delegating a lot to him anyway recently. Go off and email me that document. Oh, and not that it matters, but any change on the Scotland position? Are they feeling any more British these days?

BRIAN: Well they're quite opposed to it, as I said.

ROGER: No change then.

BRIAN: They're all opposed to it – Wales, Northern Ireland

ROGER: Why?

BRIAN: They don't like

ROGER: Each other?

BRIAN: No

ROGER: What about England?

BRIAN: Oh, no, they're fine.

ROGER: They're still for it?

BRIAN: Yes.

ROGER: And do FIFA approve of that?

BRIAN: They do

ROGER: So England can represent Britain in the Olympic football competition?

BRIAN: Yes, that's the way it looks

ROGER: You know what Brian in spite of your let downs I think we might just win this

15B. THE DAMASCUS ROAD MOMENT

BRIAN: I don't think so.

ROGER: What?

BRIAN: I think it would be better if we lost.

ROGER: I'm sorry?

BRIAN: Well we're a very small country with a rather large ego and winning might actually throw it out of control. I really think it would be a lot better if we sort of lost. Heroically.

ROGER: I'm confused. We didn't spend all this money in order to come second.

BRIAN: Or worse.

ROGER: This is a country –

BRIAN: I know what you're going to say

ROGER: What?

BRIAN: Harry Potter, The Beatles, David Beckham's right foot.

BRIAN moves over to beneath the microphone which had been used for the media announcement at the beginning – not that it's on yet.

ROGER: David Beckham's left foot, the Henley Regatta, Wensleydale cheese, Take That, Scott of the Antarctic

BRIAN: Charge of the Light Brigade. Maureen Lipman. Alan Bennett…

ROGER: …old maids cycling through the morning mist to mass

BRIAN: Come friendly bombs and fall on Slough/ it isn't fit for humans now…

ROGER: Milton Keynes, Exeter, Telford, Warrington, Toxteth, *, pigeon fanciers, bingo callers, shoppers, a whole nation of **shed dwelling losers** *(cue to cut BRIAN's recitation.)* Oh

BRIAN: *(Simultaneous from *.)* This is the night mail crossing the border, bringing the cheque and the postal order. Miss Joan Hunter Dunn, Miss Joan Hunter Dunn, she sat in the car park til twenty to one and now I'm engaged to Miss Joan Hunter Dunn.

Silence.

BRIAN: Well we'll have to see what happens in the match I suppose

BLACKOUT.

In the blackout the stage is transformed into a desolate office in the midst of being disbanded – archive boxes litter the floor.

16. LAST DAYS OF THE DCMS

BRIAN: Do you think I'll still get the pay rise?

NIGEL: No mate.

BRIAN: Performance related pay rise.

NIGEL: No, mate, no. No mate.

BRIAN: Roger told me it was guaranteed.

NIGEL: No mate.

BRIAN: We stood to make a lot of money out of this.

NIGEL: No, mate. No.

BRIAN: Well, that's the only reason I did it.

NIGEL: Well, its irrelevant now isn't it?

BRIAN: I think we've got to forget this whole thing about Britain, don't you think?

NIGEL: Yeah, but look what happened in the former Yugoslavia

BRIAN: What do you mean?

NIGEL: I dunno, mate, I'm working in the tax department now so I'm just winding up affairs really.

NIGEL goes off to pack his box.

BRIAN: Do you think we should have employed a sports psychologist?

NIGEL: That's what Sir Alex is.

BRIAN: A hypnotist?

NIGEL: *You* might need a psychologist.

BRIAN: A hypnotist – next time, well there won't be a next time will there? God, we always get it wrong, don't we, when we imagine the future. You know why? Well I know.

NIGEL: *(Appearing from behind the boxes.)* Hang on let me try and answer you. Give me a chance

BRIAN: You're going to get it wrong.

NIGEL: Look at Zidane's headbutt yeah? – you know, yeah? The reason he did that is not anything to do with Matterrazzi calling his mother an Algerian whore yeah? – nothing to do with that , it's all about – cos he visualized glory yeah? This gifted man – he'd scored two headers in the previous world cup final , you know, beautiful goals against Brazil, the best team in the history of football yeah? And so the moment comes – This is against Italy four years later – There's a few minutes left of extra time, ball comes across, he rises, bang, beautiful header towards the goal, on target, Bouffon saves it, yeah the script is ripped up yeah didn't work, like he imagined yeah? He visualized, didn't happen yeah? No glory yeah? And that's why he lost it – rage, head butt

BRIAN: It's not just the events that I'm talking about

NIGEL: Yeah... what?

BRIAN: We imagine our response and we get it wrong. Same with having children. We think they're going to make us happy, but they don't. You know why?

NIGEL: *(Appearing at front again but now with Spiv coat and bag.)* What? Nappies?

BRIAN: Because we imagine it through the eyes of the present. We should go to somebody who's been in a high profile match and had a big win and ask them if it made them happy. Who's been in that position?

NIGEL: Spain, France, Brazil, Italy,

BRIAN: Let's go to Italy, well its too late now. We should have gone to Italy

NIGEL: *(Re-entering having finished packing.)* I'm off Bri

BRIAN: But it's important. I need to show everyone that it's actually all right to lose. That I was right.

NIGEL: I'm going to be working on inheritance tax

BRIAN: You can't leave me alone like this, we've got all these papers, all these match reports I don't understand half of it

NIGEL: I've cleared my desk

BRIAN: What the fuck am I gonna do? I've got to meet the prime minister at 4.30

NIGEL: I'm working on Inheritance, Bri. I'm sorry.

BRIAN: No you're not, you're an EO.

NIGEL: Eh?

BRIAN: You're an EO, aren't you?

NIGEL: Not any more, mate.

BRIAN: What d'you mean?

NIGEL: I'm gonna be a Grade 7. Grade 7. Grade 7.

BRIAN: Please stop saying that.

NIGEL: Grade 7?

BRIAN: Stop it.

NIGEL: Stop saying EO EO. You sound like a donkey.

BRIAN: Well you sound like a cat.

NIGEL: I thought you liked cats. *(Mimicking a cat.)* Grade 7. Grade 7. Grade 7.

BRIAN: So how come?

NIGEL: I got the temporary promotion. Acting HEO. Then I was fast tracked and made a *(Mimicking cat.)* grade 7 – your wife did the interview actually – Amanda, isn't it?

Pause.

NIGEL: She's a bit of alright.

BRIAN: This isn't right / It's not fair.

NIGEL: There's no lines anymore Bri.

BRIAN: I did all the groundwork. You just waltzed in.

NIGEL: You were the centre forward, but you didn't score any goals. The ball came to you.

BRIAN: Can you leave out all this football?

NIGEL: The creative people, the playmakers, like myself, are being protected and used in the most effective roles. I'm going to number ten.

BRIAN: Are you calling me uncreative?

NIGEL: I said to Peter Crouch after the game – what would you be if you weren't a footballer?

BRIAN: Peter Crouch?

NIGEL: Yeah he said – a virgin *(Beat.)* then he started doing his robot dance

NIGEL: Bye, Brian.

BRIAN: Where are you going? Nigel, you can't leave me and go away and be a grade whatsit without me.

NIGEL: Are you being racialist? You think I'm a piccaninny? You think I'm a piccaninny? It's good to have met you mate. Good to have worked with you

BRIAN: What am I gonna do? I've got to ring somebody – who? There's no one left. Their jobs have been deleted.

NIGEL: Good luck mate. No hard feelings. Did you hear Roger Jeffreys got made redundant?

NIGEL becomes MIGGY and appears with a furniture removal trolley to start taking away boxes to the dump.

BRIAN: Fucking football. Shoulder feint. *(Laughs.)* Nutmegs. I've been nutmegged.

MIGGY: *(BRIAN starts crying.)* I know it's terrible. When you see your team lose. We cried for a week once. There was nothing we could do. *(Pause as BRIAN cries.).* Country fell apart. It was a disaster. I had to leave Algiers – leave the country.

BRIAN: I thought you were an economic migrant?

MIGGY: No – I'm a refugee – a soccer refugee – like Escobar should have been – but he went back to Columbia after the own goal in USA '94 and they shot him – 6 times in the face and every time the fired the gun – the gunman do you know what he said? 'goal' 'goal' 'goal' 'goal' 'goal' 'goal' … You'll be ok, you're not getting shot in the face – literally. You don't have to leave or anything. I'll get you a mint tea. A little mint tea makes everything better.

BRIAN: My job's over. Everything's over.

MIGGY: Think of the game. The beautiful game.

BRIAN: But it wasn't beautiful, was it?

MIGGY: It was almost beautiful.

BRIAN: Did you see it?

MIGGY: What about the little guy? – When he went through the play. *(Demonstrates.)* Moved through 4 places. And then pow!

BRIAN: What's that?

MIGGY: It was one of the most beautiful goals. Mobility, humility, sexy, beautiful... It was almost like a bird with his feet like that

BRIAN: That was the other side.

MIGGY: Oh.

BRIAN: We didn't score any goals.

MIGGY: The jerseys. They change and it's so confusing. One day they change, is it a home game? Is it an away game or the third change strip? I get confused. *(He notices BRIAN is crying and sings to him Jaques Brelle style with accompaniment.)* And did those feet, in ancient time, walk upon England mountain green, and was the holy lamb of god on England pleasant pasture seen,

BRIAN joins in with harmony line.

and did the countenance divine, *(MIGGY does voice trumpet accompaniment as BRIAN continues singing.)* shine forth upon our clouded hills *(They duet again.)* and was Jerusalem builded here, among these dark satanic mills

MIGGY: La cucaracha, la cucaracha, la da da da da da, Poque no tiene, poque le falta, ya da der der der da.... It's Marijuana. I'll get some music

MIGGY accidentally bangs into the wall with his trolley and the office walls fall inwards, BRIAN miraculously saved because he remembers the Buster Keaton film and subconsciously reproduces one of the greatest and most dangerous stunts in the entire history of silent cinema.

18. FACE DOWN IN THE CANAL

ROGER sitting in his fishing chair, BRIAN checking the end of his line downstage.

ROGER: Did you catch anything?

BRIAN: Nothing.

BRIAN walks back to his chair.

ROGER: I caught a boot once – and they reckoned err it was the original one Michael Owen scored against Argentina with in the 98 world cup

BRIAN: Did they?

ROGER: Yeah

BRIAN: But they didn't prove it?

ROGER: The authenticity was a bit of an issue when I tried to auction it on ebay

BRIAN: You just dropped a t then

ROGER: Did I? I beg your pardon

BRIAN: That's alright

ROGER: Finally. *(Silence.)* About everything that happened in the DCMS

BRIAN: It's alright Roger.

ROGER: Water under the bridge.

BRIAN: How's Ronaldo doing now? You don't hear much of him now that he's gone to Portugal

ROGER: Real Madrid?

BRIAN: Don't hear much of him now.

ROGER: Yeah you'd have to go to Madrid.

BRIAN: Yeah? Maybe I should go to Madrid then.

ROGER: Apparently there's good fishing in Spain.

BRIAN: I was reading about him the other day when he was in Manchester. He was a fan of that band with the brothers in. What are they called?

ROGER: White Stripes?

BRIAN: No, no, no. With those two brothers in – Gallaghers.

ROGER: Oh. Oasis.

BRIAN: Yeah, he was a fan of Oasis, Ronaldo.

ROGER: I thought you were going to say The Proclaimers then.

BRIAN: No, no, he was a fan of Oasis.

ROGER: *(Sings.)* – If you go will you send back a letter from Real Madrid.

BRIAN: Yeah, 'cos I was reading in his autobiography.

ROGER: Oh did he write it himself?

BRIAN: I don't know, it sounds like he might have done, so simply written. It's called 'Moments.'

ROGER: You wouldn't expect a writer to score brilliant goals like he does so why would you expect a goal scorer like him to write a brilliant book?

BRIAN: He might have. It's called 'Moments.'

ROGER: Yeah so was it a good read?

BRIAN: Well he was going on in that or in the newspaper about how he was a fan of Oasis and that he had a chance to meet one of them and he said that Liam or whoever it was didn't look at him and didn't even say anything to him. And Ronaldo's comment was 'Yes, but you know what they're like, these creative types.'

ROGER: No. It's because they're Manchester City fans.

(BRIAN: You know what they're like, these creative types.)

ROGER: So – he didn't think of himself as creative?

BRIAN: Obviously not. So what is he then?

ROGER: He's a sportsman. They play by rules. Creative types don't play by rules.

BRIAN: He's creative in his modeling for D and G ....
Someone was watching us just then –

ROGER: Hey?

SFX – dogs and dog calling – BRIAN and ROGER look out.

BRIAN: Somebody with two dogs – *(Shouts.)* Stay away from our fish

ROGER: I hate it, I hate when people walk along canals talking – don't they realize that, you know, this is an art form and it requires concentration?

BRIAN: Yes, it does.

ROGER: On both the part of the angler and the fish

BRIAN: It's a bit like meditating.

Pause.

I often wonder what it would be like if I didn't have a frontal lobe – then I'd never be worried, would I?

ROGER: You'd be an animal – you'd go around ravaging things –the frontal lobe is reason, is basically evolution. Yes it arrived between the cavemen and now. The frontal lobe arrived and look what it's brought us – what has it brought us? Eh? Happiness?

BRIAN: Without the frontal lobe I'd have no concept of the future, so if you said to me can you go and get that football from the other room – I'd go into the other room, and there'd be nothing there. And if you said to me are we going to win the football at the two thousand and twelve Olympics I'd have no idea what you were talking about 'cos I couldn't conceive of the future in two thousand and twelve – if I had no frontal lobe. All I can conceive of is the next couple of seconds – I could anticipate the end of your sentences but that would be it.

ROGER: and then you would…Fall asleep

BRIAN: …and fart. Sounds quite attractive.

Pause.

Have you got a drill?

ROGER: I've got my fish knife.

BRIAN: I was reading an article in The Guardian the other day about people who drill a hole in their head and get a permanent high? Surely you'd get used to a permanent high and you'd want to get a high on top of it wouldn't you?

ROGER: Yeah I reckon sooner or later you'd end up as a miserable git, bit like Fabio Capello

BRIAN: Interesting yeah… Is he?

ROGER: Well he is now, after what happened…

BRIAN: I was in Japan once. I picked up a fungal toe infection.

ROGER: You told me.

BRIAN: Mind you, it's gone now 'cos I've been taking the tablets that are destroying my liver and causing chronic flatulence that keeps me awake at night.

ROGER: Look at us now.

BRIAN: What?

ROGER: Look at us now.

BRIAN: It's true, my flatulence is so bad it keeps me awake. I can't sleep, I fart all night

ROGER: Serious?

BRIAN: I looked up the side effects of these tablets, but it doesn't mention flatulence. Think I have to phone up the company and say look I found a new side effect – chronic flatulence. Only during the night.

Pause.

ROGER: How's Amanda?

BRIAN: She's pregnant. And I'm fine about it now really, the donor thing. But in moments of quiet reflection I can't help wondering how I will feel watching my son score for Britain or win the Booker prize or Britain's Got Talent, more likely. Will I feel a swell of parental pride or will I sit there thinking that my son is only achieving these things because I am not his father.

ROGER: Well, thanks for the heads up.

BRIAN: What does that actually mean?

ROGER: Its where, you know – you make sure everyone is singing from the same hymn sheet. There was another post mortem piece in the paper claiming that by finishing in the last 16, which everyone thinks is a disaster actually represents an overachievement – based on GDP, population, and experience and – we should be celebrating as heroic losers – that'd galvanise Britain.

BRIAN: We can't talk about football forever.

ROGER: The reason why we avoid talking about anything but football is cos we can't – we're just clichéd men , British men, English men. Can't talk about their personal feelings and emotions. So we talk about football instead.

Pause.

How are you feeling?

BRIAN: I'm not feeling good about football.

ROGER: Good yes – talk about your feelings about football as opposed to football – maybe that's a way for us to open up about our feelings by talking about our feelings about football.

BRIAN: I was just a bit fed up with the obsessive coverage, that's all. Within myself I'm fine.

ROGER: Do you want to talk about it?

BRIAN: No.

ROGER: No? No I don't want to talk about it either. Just one day you will find me floating face down in the canal.

BRIAN: Why?

ROGER: Because I had nobody to talk to. And yet here we are..

BRIAN: You're talking to me, what you talking about?

ROGER: I know we're getting onto it now, but we don't want to do it do we? We don't want to. You know I said: 'Do you want to talk about your feelings?' You said 'No I don't' and I said 'Neither do I' and then I'll be face down in the canal

BRIAN: *(He cries.)* You laughing or crying? I don't mind the feelings coming out but I don't want this organized: 'Let's sit down and talk about our feelings' thing . That's what puts me off, if you know what I mean – Alright mate? Yeah?

ROGER: Did you just try and comfort me with your fishing rod?

Snap blackout.

THE END.

www.ingramcontent.com/pod-product-compliance
Ingram Content Group UK Ltd.
Pitfield, Milton Keynes, MK11 3LW, UK
UKHW020729280225
455688UK00012B/572